Don't Forget Your Customers!

Don't Forget Your Customers!

A Marketing Guide for Small Businesses

Vicki Lenz

Louisville, Kentucky

Library of Congress Catalog Card Number: 96-96150

ISBN 0-9651641-0-1

Edited by Patti Parsons
Cover and book design by Sue Dawson

ATTENTION ASSOCIATIONS AND ORGANIZATIONS: Quantity discounts are available on bulk purchases of this book. Special books or book excerpts can also be created to fit specific needs. For information, please contact Affordable Marketing Co., 8206 Lacevine Rd., Louisville, Kentucky 40220, or call/fax (502) 495-1361.

Note to Readers

Over my years as a marketing consultant to small businesses, I frequently encountered owners that were spending hundreds and thousands of dollars - on ad campaigns, mailers, phone book advertising, and so on - to attract new customers. I wrote this book, in part, because of my sometimes-frustrating experiences with business people that insist on spending their hard earned money trying to appeal to prospects - while ignoring the gold mine that they already have right under their noses - existing customers! Don't get me wrong. I know that part of the battle is to get your message out and win over new customers. In my marketing management positions for both large and small companies, mass marketing to attract new customers was what I practiced and preached.

But I've learned from experience, and see that there is indeed another (and better) way to grow a business. And that is conducting business to gain more "share of customer" rather than "share of market." It's exciting to me when a small business recognizes and practices marketing to customers, and is thrilled with the results. I'm happy to bring together this information in a how-to format to help you. Many business owners were more than willing to share their experiences, and I'm pleased to present these examples because I believe we all learn from each other.

"Share of Customer" vs. "Market Share"

I've seen and read a lot of books on marketing, and you could probably find a marketing-related seminar to attend any day of the week. Several books presented certain elements of a customer-focused program that really got me thinking. One book in particular, *The One To One Future: Building Relationships One Customer at a Time*, by Don Peppers and Martha Rogers, Ph.D., opened my eyes to "share of customer" marketing. But I couldn't find any one source that I thought wrapped everything together in a logical approach for small businesses. So, that's what I've done with Don't Forget Your Customers! It's not a detailed, jargon-filled, ultimate resource. Instead, it's an easy and quick read (since we're all busy trying to run our businesses) designed to give you some basic and simple ideas to begin applying to your business.

And there's another reason. When was the last time you were really 'wowed' by a buying experience, or truly felt appreciated as a customer? I recently had the occasion to hire a plumber to do some work around our house. On the day of the appointment, he called first to let me know that he was on his way. He arrived on time. He did exactly was he was supposed to do, and on the low side of the price range that I was originally quoted. He showed me his work upon completion and explained what had been done and why. He gave me tips about things I could do myself without having to call a plumber. He was very professional. I

Surprise Me!

later received a thank you note in the mail. Afterwards, I started thinking about what a pleasant experience it was - which then made me wonder. Why can't we (as customers) come to expect this as the norm, rather than an exception? Will I recommend his company to friends and relatives, and use their services again in the future? Definitely!

Be the exception, not the norm. Treat customers the way you want to be treated. My hope is that by reading this book, you'll start thinking about running your business in a customer-focused environment to create lifetime customers and reap the benefits. Marketing to your customers is an exciting and fun way to do business, and a win-win situation for everyone.

Don't Forget Your Customers!
A Marketing Guide for Small Businesses

Table of Contents

Introduction

When I mentioned a "marketing to your customers strategy" to small business owner Don Morgan, his eyes lit up, and he couldn't wait to share his recent experience along those lines. Don's photography studio, in business for 25 years, had been successful by relying on a few traditional marketing methods: Yellow Pages advertising, some direct mail campaigns from purchased lists, and word-of-mouth from satisfied customers. Then one day, for an anniversary celebration, Don decided to send a special offer only to customers that had used his services within the past sixteen months. For a cost of under $300, Don brought in sales over $25,000! This is only one of many success stories you'll read about in this book.

Marketing by focusing on your existing customers is a way of doing business. It's a combination of elements - formed into a working strategy - that produce both immediate and long term positive results. It's a strategy based on developing loyal, lifetime customers by striving for "share of customer" rather than "share of market." The focus is on customers, which all businesses need to survive.

It's a way of doing business

When I shared my "don't forget your customers" concept with a table full of business people at a recent Chamber of Commerce meeting, it was fun to watch reactions as the simpleness of the idea sank in. After all, this is not rocket science. It's fundamental to doing business, but not something we consciously think about developing. As one business owner shared, "I walk past my file cabinets (full of past customer records) almost every day, but never really thought about the potential that they represent. Instead, I've spent a lot of time and money trying to attract more and more new customers."

Why didn't I think of that?

It doesn't matter if your small business sells products or services, or your customers are consumers or businesses, marketing by focusing on existing customers can work for you. This book is for and about small businesses (whatever your definition), since we usually don't have the big budgets, in-house marketing staff, or ad agencies that large companies do. We may be great at providing our product or service, but lack the time, money, know-how, or staff for marketing. Or maybe we're just looking for a better way.

Is this book for you?

This way of marketing is for all of you who have spent hundreds or thousands on advertising, with less than desirable results. It's for companies with or without sales staff. It's for companies that have been around for a long time, with lots of customers, that just want to make sure they're prepared for the future. It's for companies losing long-time customers to competitors. It's for those of you thinking about developing a customer-focused program. It's helpful to those of you with new businesses, in designing a marketing program to get you off to the right start and plan for the future.

Examples provided in this book are from a combination of sources. Some are my own personal or business experiences and ideas. Others are merely my observations of what works for big businesses that can be adapted by small businesses. Many others are stories and examples kindly shared by small business owners and friends, to which I am eternally grateful - and you should be too! Feel free to "borrow" and adapt them to your business.

Steal some ideas!

I sincerely believe you'll find something in this book that makes sense for your business, and that you can't wait to try. Happy customer-focused marketing!

Chapter 1

Why You Shouldn't Forget Your Customers

Would you rather have five customers that make one-time purchases, or one customer that remains loyal and keeps coming back (i.e., spending more money with you)? Chances are that you're reading this book because you believe that the second choice is the best choice for the long-term success of your business. It's just that we tend to forget about our existing customers! If you think about it, there are lots of common sense reasons for focusing marketing efforts on your existing customers - we just need to be reminded of the benefits:

Customers are a company's best asset

- Research shows that it costs five times more (at least) to land a new customer than to keep a customer you already have.

- It's easier to sell because they already know you.

- It strengthens your position in the market place, because loyal customers are coming back to you instead of buying from your competition.

Common-sense benefits

- It can reduce your marketing costs, such as advertising, because your sales force is expanding as satisfied customers tell their friends and relatives about you and do your selling for you.

- It can insulate you somewhat from price competition - as long as you're fair and treat customers right, they'll be less likely to shop competition solely on price.

Increase sales and profits

- Customers will be more likely to try other products and services that you have to offer.

- All businesses need customers to survive!

- And, customers are your best source for what's really going on in the market place and how your business can continue to meet their needs.

What I'm revealing here is not an amazing new discovery, nor is it extremely complicated. Remembering your customers is a simple idea that we seem to forget about in our daily struggle to survive in the business world. What I am presenting is an organized approach for developing a company culture and program to focus on customers. It's both the big and little elements that, when combined, form a strategy that seeks to develop loyal, lifetime customers. It's striving for more "share of customer" rather than "share of market."

"Must Have" Elements for Long Term Success

I hope any or all of these reasons are enough to capture your interest, so that you'll proceed to learn what it takes to focus on your customers. However, there are a few "must have" elements for making this type of program work. You might get by on a short-term basis without having all these elements, but your best bet for continued, long-term success means buying into all of them.

- You must first be offering quality products and services, with a solid support system.

- Management has to believe in the program and lead by example. All phases of your business should be operating with a customer-focused mindset and attitude.

An organized approach

- Everyone in the company, no matter what position, should not only understand the program, but be actively involved and entrusted.

- It will be necessary to understand, use and embrace technology. Be ready to adapt to the future.

- Put your plan of action in writing, spelling out your strategy to keep customers and get more of their business.

- Customer appreciation programs should be a continuous part of your strategy.

- Recognize that this is not a "quick fix." Patience is required to see the results. Remember, your goal is to have customers for life!

- Strong ethics and values must be an integral part of the way you do business. Long term relationships are built on trust.

Too good to be true!

Let me share an experience with you that I think represents a very ethical, customer-focused approach. Back-yard bird watching is one of my hobbies. I especially enjoy hummingbirds, and I know they're attracted to misting water. I had rigged up a hose with a standard spray nozzle on the end, because I didn't want to pay $50 for the special nozzle available locally. Then I spotted a small classified ad in one of my birding magazines. For $15 (including shipping and handling), there was the promise of a simple water mister, an ultra-low volume nozzle that produces a fine spray mist to attract birds to drink and leaf bathe. It was one of those 'sounds too good to be true' situations. I debated for a week before ordering, wondering if I'd be sending my check into oblivion someplace in Florida. Then, surprise! Less than two weeks later, I received a small brown padded envelope from SIMPLE MISTER. Inside was a quality water mister, as promised. Also inside was a one-page sheet providing very helpful suggestions for use. At the bottom of the sheet was the following hand-written note:

"Mrs. Lenz: We made an improvement and actually lowered our cost. Please find $2.05 enclosed."

And there was a separate envelope with $2.05 in cash enclosed! Talk about a nice surprise. And the mister worked as promised! When I later talked to owner Chip Cunningham, he explained that this way of doing business was "just my nature." How wonderfully refreshing. As for the other facets of marketing, Chip shared that he was just starting out, and the classified ads (fairly inexpensive) in that one publication were his first effort in paid advertising. He's receiving a decent response. But look what he managed to generate in new business through our transaction: I purchased two more nozzles for friends (friends will tell more friends); I highly recommend the nozzle to anyone who asks; I'm a customer for life; and SIMPLE MISTER is getting free publicity in this book!

When I mention the word marketing, what comes to mind? Advertising? Sales representatives? Direct mail? Telephone sales? I won't bore you with dictionary definitions of marketing; instead I'll share my interpretation and vision. First, what marketing is NOT. It is not just advertising, sales reps, direct mail, or telemarketing. It is not just a promotion to attract new customers. It is not something to be done periodically (like when sales are down), by whatever means look good at the time. Marketing IS a way of doing business. It's a whole program of

What is marketing?

things and it's not any single item. It includes how you service, retain, and appreciate customers. (The term "customer" is "one that buys goods or services." Feel free to substitute the common term in your business, such as client, patron, shopper, etc.) Marketing is an important investment in your business. We need customers in order to survive. If you're in business, you're already doing some marketing, or you wouldn't have any customers. Just be ready to open your mind to what may be a new or different vision of marketing.

A way of doing business

The Most Effective Approach for Small Businesses

Actually, this approach works for any size business. But I've written this book and designed this program specifically for small businesses. Big businesses have marketing departments, advertising budgets, highly paid advisers, and bureaucracy! That doesn't necessarily mean that they recognize the value of customer-focused marketing or conduct business accordingly. Small business owners have several advantages in this area. Why? They generally are more flexible, creative, and eager to learn and implement new ideas. They can readily make changes and adapt. It's quicker and easier for a small business to see results. I believe that they tend to think twice about spending hard earned dollars on a mass marketing advertising campaign (or hope

It's cost-effective

they will after reading this book). And, I think small business owners tend to be closer to the customers and understand what it is to be a customer. They truly want to choose a course of action that makes sense for everyone.

TIPS

T
I
P
S

- *Do a Reality Check. All the great marketing in the world won't help if you're not providing quality products/services that someone needs. Before you decide marketing is the answer, take an objective, overall look at your business and your goals.*

- *And, very simple but often ignored, my "Golden Rule of Customer-Focused Marketing":* **Treat each customer the way you want to be treated as a customer.**

Chapter 2

What's ONE Customer Worth?

Recognizing Lifetime Values

It's time to take a look at your customers
and get to know them individually. You
probably already know the general information about your customers and can
group them into various categories relative
to your type of business. Now here's the big
question: What's a single customer worth to
your business over a lifetime?

Say you're selling widgets, and XYZ Company buys $5,000 of widget type-A in one
year. Very simply put, buying widget type-A
over a 20-year period could mean $100,000
in revenue from XYZ Company. (In twenty
years you intend to sell your business and
retire wealthy!) However, you also sell
type-B through Z widgets, and XYZ Company uses some of those types too — but
they're buying them from a competitor.
What would the value of customer XYZ
Company be over a lifetime if they were
buying all the widgets they needed from you?

*More of
each
customer's
dollars -
long term*

Let's use an example from car dealer Carl
Sewell's book, *Customers for Life*. Carl
estimates a potential lifetime value for each
customer at $332,000. That's the price of

twelve cars they'll buy in a lifetime, including all the parts and service work that go
along with it. There's also the ripple effect.
For every referral sent your way by a
happy customer, there's an opportunity to
gain another $332,000 in lifetime sales.

Of course, you can't know for certain what
an individual customer will buy from you
over the next month, much less over the
next 20 or 30 years. But there are ways to
estimate, such as asking the customer to
tell you (via ways discussed in future
chapters), or making predictions based on
that customer's past behavior and histori-
cal records.

***People and
situations
change***

Even if you think you're providing a one-
time service or product, think again. Don't
forget that you're dealing with individuals.
People will spread the word to others,
whether bragging or cursing. People move
and change jobs. What someone didn't need
yesterday, they might need tomorrow.
Conditions change, and there are always
new opportunities. It may be difficult to
attach an estimated dollar amount to each
customer, but at least recognize that in
some way, a customer for life has plenty of
potential value.

***Customers
won't
automatically
remember
you***

Say you're an architect or building contrac-
tor, hired by an owner to design or build a
new building. Once that particular project
is over, there's still the potential for future
business. Remodeling or additions may be
necessary in the future, or even an entirely

new building. The owner or staff that you worked with during that project may move on to another facility needing your services. Subcontractors that had a good experience working with you won't hesitate to recommend you on other projects. You see, there are opportunities, but besides recognizing them, you must also communicate with customers and have ongoing dialog. Don't rely on the fact that you did a good job and assume that they'll think about you in the future. We don't have great memories, hence "out of sight - out of mind."

No matter what your business, there's a potential lifetime value for customers; you may just need to see things in a different light. Now that's not saying that every customer is a lifetime customer. Have you discovered your best customers? Generally, 20% of your customers are producing 80% of your revenues. In different industries the percentages will vary, but whatever the percentages, there is some difference among customers that makes some of them more valuable than others. Given the potential value of those 20%-type customers, doesn't it make sense to have a marketing approach designed just for them?

The 80/20 rule

TIP
T
I
P

Open your mind to see customers differently. What you might have perceived as a one-time sale may represent a lifetime value.

Chapter 3

Let's Communicate!

In mass marketing, the task is selling to as many people as possible, and the strategy and promotion is designed to get your message to the target masses and increase market share. You're not concerned with the needs of each customer, only with the total numbers of customers and sales. Now, instead of the mass marketing mentality, I want you to think about communicating with each customer to learn and meet their needs. Think in terms of increasing your share of each customer's patronage, not in terms of your company's share of market. It doesn't matter if you have 5 customers or 15,000, it's still do-able. Okay, this is different. It's not the traditional way of marketing. But do you really want to stay traditional? As fast as things are changing, don't you owe it to your company to see things differently? My well-founded fear (and it should be yours too) is that companies which continue to do business with the attitude "here's what we've got - take it or leave it" won't be around very long.

2-way dialog with EACH customer

When you strive for "share of customer," that means ensuring that each individual customer who buys your product/service buys more, buys only yours, is happy with your product/service, and stays as a lifetime customer. When you strive for "market

share," that means selling as much of your
product/service as you can to as many
people as you can. Now, which way do you
think will be more beneficial in the long
run?

Gathering Information

*Who are
your
customers?*

How do you get to know each customer
(and find that 20%-type)? If you're a very
small business with a limited number of
customers, this may not be a problem for
you. If you have lots of customers, you need
to maintain some basic information and
find ways to get them to identify themselves - individually. How many customers
who started with you last year are still
buying this year? Which ones have stayed
with you over the years? How much are
they spending with you, and on which
products or services? What's their frequency of purchase?

Plan ahead

What records do you already have? Is there
some way to link identities to transactions?
Here's where a computer is essential. Start
building your own database of customer
information. The type of information that
you'll need to gather and maintain will
depend on your type of business and customers, but here are some areas ("fields" in
database language) you may want to choose
from. Remember, plan for the future when
setting up your database; try to anticipate
the type of information you may need.

• business name
• customer name

- title
- company
- mailing address
- facility address
- phone number - office/home
- pager or portable phone number
- fax number
- e-mail address
- product/service currently purchasing
- last purchase date
- future needs/potential
- contact dates/description
- proposal/project status
- customer since (date)
- customer type
- average sale (type or $)
- sales transactions and dates
- follow-up dates
- referred by

Some of the methods of communication identified in the following section can also be utilized to gather information about your customers. Imagine, for example, that you sell computers and want to start offering installation and set-up services for in-home business and personal use, but you don't know which customers are purchasing them for such use. For computers sold over the next month, you could could sponsor a contest and give away a set-up service to a different winner each week. In order to enter the contest, customers have to complete your brief survey form. On the survey form, ask for the basic contact information, along with a few qualifying questions that

Multiple uses

could help you determine if this is a viable service for your customers.

Opening Lines of Communication

Listen to your customers

Once you have some basic information on your loyal customers, it's time to start communicating with them on a one-to-one basis. Why, you ask? 1) Because in order to continue to get their business, and get more of it, you have to know their needs, their likes and dislikes. 2) Because you need feedback on how you're performing and if you are indeed meeting their needs. 3) Because you have to start building a relationship with them. Remember how word-of-mouth advertising and referrals work? We prefer to do business with someone we know, trust, or that has been recommended to us. Your best relationships will define your best customers, and your most profitable business. Are you beginning to get the picture?

Imagine the small town general store of yesteryear. In their book *The One to One Future*, Don Peppers and Martha Rogers present the example of the general store proprietor that knew every one of his customers. He knew which groceries Mrs. Smith needed, and that her family's tastes and groceries were different from that of her neighbor. If Mrs. Smith suddenly stopped buying a certain item, the grocer would notice and try to find the reason for the change. Maybe her doctor recommended a new diet, or she was shopping somewhere else. The grocer's business was built on relationships with his customers. He remembered the important things about each customer, which allowed him to solve problems for them and continue to meet their changing needs. In return, he increased his business with the lifetime value of each customer.

Of course, your business is probably not the general store. But the basic concept is the same. There are a variety of ways that you can open lines of communication with your customers. Again, the methods you choose will depend on your type of business and customer base size. Here are a few to get you started thinking. You will want to mix and match, use methods in combination with each other (like surveys and contests), and choose as many as make sense for your business. Be creative, and don't limit your selection to what's typical for your industry. You'll find how various businesses are applying (or could apply) some of these methods in Chapters 6 and 7.

Build long-term relationships

- **In Person**
  The best salespeople that I know are successful because they listen to the needs of the individual and figure out how to meet those needs, rather than just try to promote their goods.

- **MBWA** *(Management By Walking Around)*
  Rather than sitting in the back room of

your store or hiding out in the ivory tower, go out in the real world. Walk around and observe, listen, talk to your customers and your competition's customers.

Mix and match

- **Informal Focus Groups**
  Invite a small group of your customers to lunch. Go prepared with a brief agenda that keys in on a few elements of your product or service, and ask what they like, dislike, or how they would change it.

- **Surveys**
  A simple two or three question survey, in person or by phone or mail, can help you determine if customers are pleased with your business, or give you ideas for changes.

- **Contests**
  Have a contest open to your customers to help promote a particular product or service, and combine the entry form with a brief survey or questionnaire.

- **Complaints**
  Listen, solve the problem, and learn. Valid complaints are signals that changes need to be made in your business.

- **Direct Mail** (i.e., post cards, surveys, flyers, letters, brochures, newsletters, and thank-you notes)
  Any of these can be used to communicate with your customers and encourage their

response and input. Written materials should identify easy ways for your customer to contact you. They might include fax numbers, e-mail addresses, 800 numbers, or a tear-off return card or coupon.

- **Telephone** (i.e., 800 numbers, hold messages, and voice mail)
Be accessible and make it as easy as possible for the customer to communicate with you. If you have a lot of long-distance customers, don't give them reason to seek out a competitor because you don't have an 800 number. If you must put customers on hold, consider hold messages that introduce them to your other products or services, educate, or explain benefits. Voice mail can allow customers to leave short or long messages, and enable them to reach you at hours convenient to them.

Use a lot of different methods

- **Fax on Demand**
This is a relatively new technology allowing callers to immediately receive information from you via fax. What you fax back could be coupons, details about your product or service, or perhaps a survey or order form.

- **Computer** (i.e., bar-coding, e-mail, home page on the Web)
Costs are coming down, more people are computer-efficient, and these methods are not so highly technical or costly anymore. Bar-coding and scanning

products can help you learn the buying
preferences of each customer. E-mail
(electronic mail) encourages quick and
clear communication. A home page on
the Web (your business "address" and
information on the World Wide Web)
makes it easy for a customer to learn
more about your business, at their
leisure. It can even allow them to actually make purchases, or complete a
survey form. Plus, you can "link" with
other related pages that you know would
be of interest to your customers. (Read
more about the Web later in this chapter.)

- **Frequent Buyer Programs**

   These reward customers that buy more,
   like "purchase five widgets and get the
   sixth one free." What better way learn
   about your customers, keep them happy,
   and get them to spend more money with
   you?

*Act on
feedback*

Here's one example of using some of these
methods. Out of frustration, I tried a little
experiment with 800 phone numbers for
customer service. My frustration centered
on my husband's can of shaving cream,
which leaves a rust ring on the counter top.
On the other hand, my can of shaving
cream (designed for women by another
manufacturer) has a plastic no-rust ring on
the bottom. So I called the 800 number for
my husband's brand. The real person that
finally answered was nice, but merely
listened to my comment about my husband

liking their product, and suggestion for a no-rust ring. I was thanked for my comments; end of conversation. Did I just waste my time? Then I called the 800 number for my brand. Although I was put on hold for a short period of time, the hold message about their other consumer products was informative. When I was connected with a real person, her manner came across as someone that was really interested in my comments (versus the previous person that came across as someone just doing a job). After listening to my comments and suggestions, she explained how they would handle or act on them. To show their thanks, if I would give my name and mailing address, they would gladly send me coupons for their various products.

In the case of the second 800 number, what did the company accomplish? With their hold message, since I was a captive audience and already a customer for one product, they introduced me to some of their other products that I probably never would have even thought about. With their *Same* friendly, customer-focused attitude, they *methods,* made me feel welcome and appreciated as a *different* customer. By taking my name and address, *results* they now have some real information on me as an individual customer, not just a nameless consumer. And by sending me coupons, they've encourage me to try some of their other products, and continue to buy the product that I already like - but next time at a discount!

Granted, these were both big businesses, but the lessons and methods are applicable to small businesses as well. You can also see how similar methods (800 numbers, hold messages, direct mail, and complaints) can be utilized - but produce very different results.

Using Technology

Technology is affordable

This is no time to be a technophobe. You need to embrace some new (and some not-so-new) technologies to get the job done. Whereas the memory of the general store proprietor (who carried his database in his head) may have sufficed in the past, we must rely in part on computers today. Most of the technologies that small businesses need today to market to their customers are readily available and not that expensive. You're most likely already using some of them in your business. If so, how can you let the systems do some of the work for you?

For example, a lot of retail operations today rely on scanning bar codes on products, and utilize the information for sales and inventory management. Why not tie it into a customer information system? Computers offer plenty of opportunities for use in marketing, starting with basic word processing programs and databases. Even the telephone is a good tool, with capabilities such as voice mail, hold messages, and fax-on-demand. Again, Chapters 6 and 7 are full of examples that explain how some of these technologies can be used for marketing to your customers.

One of the fastest growing technologies predicted to change our lives and the way we conduct business is the World Wide Web. The Web enables businesses of every size - economically - to establish two-way, interactive, multi-media communications with existing and potential customers around the world. The Web is part of the Internet. The Internet is a global network of millions of computers that store a wealth of information - in boring text format. The Web allows information to be presented on your computer screen in a colorful, multimedia mixture of graphics, sound, animation, and text. The Web also allows you to access new information simply by pointing with your mouse and clicking. (It's called the World Wide Web because a chart of the crisscrossing connections among all the computers in the world looks like a giant spider web.) You can access the Web with a computer and modem through a local "server" company, or through an account with a commercial on-line services company like American Online or CompuServe. With an expenditure ranging from minor to major, your company can have a "presence" on the Web, referred to as a home page or Web site. Although the Web is generally about providing information, you can communicate with your existing and potential customers using "information" along the lines of customer service, an-

Internet and the World Wide Web

A "home page" can be many pages

nouncements, public relations, and advertisements. You can even conduct sales transactions. I personally think the jury is still out on just how effective Internet marketing can be. But if your customers tend to be computer efficient Web-browsers, this is one more way to gather information, learn their likes and dislikes, and communicate one-to-one. It's possible with your own page to have customers complete a survey form, join a preferred customer club, and even place orders. I wouldn't rely solely on this marketing platform, but it could be another piece of your customer-focused strategy.

Identifying Contact Points of Opportunity

How does a customer 'experience' your business?

Take some time now to identify all points of communication with your customers. In what way, and on what occasion, do customers come in contact with your business? Write it down, draw a picture, or start a worksheet or flow chart. There's an example worksheet on the next page. Track each point of contact with a customer from the beginning. How are phone calls received or customers greeted when they enter your place of business? How does the buying process flow? What about invoicing and follow-up? When you have the big picture laid out in front of you, ask "How (and how well) are we communicating at each point?" Remember, communication is a two-way street.

Contact Points Worksheet

Example Worksheet

Customer Contact Points	Our Process	Opportunities
REFERRAL (Heard about us from a friend)	Did we ask how they heard about us? Are we tracking results? Are we acknowledging referrals?	• Referral program
PHONE (Phoned to request information)	Was caller put on hold? Did caller have to be transferred several times before someone could help? Was information recorded in the computer database?	• Voice mail • Fax on demand • Customer-focused training for all staff
SALES VISIT (Visited by our Sales Rep)	Did Sales Rep leave literature? Does literature identify our other products and services, and their benefits?	• Conduct needs assessment
FAX & MAIL (Received quote)	Was the quote tracked? Was there any follow-up?	• Fax cover with products & services listed
PHONE (Placed order)	Was quote info readily available and used for verification, rather than making the customer repeat specs?	• Mail thank-you note • Employee training & recognition program
MAIL (Received order)	Did it ship on time? Did we enclose a new order form?	
MAIL (Received invoice)	Was a return envelope enclosed? Satisfaction survey?	
(Received no further contact from company)	None currently	• Cross-sell other products/services • Frequent Buyer program • Newsletter • Regularly scheduled sales visits • Use computer to track referrals, results, customer info, ordering & shipping info

See the big picture

You're looking at these contact areas from your viewpoint. How about experiencing your business from a customer's perspective? Since it's easy for an owner or manager to develop tunnel vision, it may be wise to hire a "mystery shopper" or independent consultant. Or treat a friend to dinner in exchange for them evaluating your business from a customer standpoint - just make sure it's someone that will be honest with you, and can view the situation objectively. You will want to know how easy it is for a customer to do business with you, and how they are encouraged to become a customer for life. Another method - if your type of business allows - is for you or one of your employees to have a customer experience with a competitor (i.e., shop the competition). Then compare the experience to your operations - with a critical eye. You might even use this for employee training. Set the scenario, and have employees role-play the part of a customer doing business with your company.

Objective viewpoint

Looking at the big picture in this manner can also help you identify the root cause of some common customer complaints, or spot internal problem areas. How does the process flow internally? Are incoming calls getting through? Does each employee understand the importance of their role in the process? Does the sales staff know what the billing department is doing? Does the outdated computer system need to be replaced?

The purpose of this exercise is to make you aware of the customer communication opportunities presented every day in your business. Your goal is to efficiently use every contact point as an opportunity. The opportunities are numerous and will overlap; use them to:

- provide the best response and customer service possible

- make it easy for customers to do business with you

- cross-sell or sell more of your products and services

Everyday possibilities

- collect information

- educate or provide information

- give customers reasons and easy ways to provide input

- learn from their input, and adjust to the needs of the customer

- "wow" your customers, surprise them, or do something totally unexpected to let them know they're appreciated

Now, extend your list, worksheet or flow chart from "the way it is now" to "the way it could be." Keep reading for ideas, and jot down thoughts and possibilities as they occur to you. Then, when you're ready to put your plan of action in writing, you'll find that your trusty worksheet (or what-ever) will show you the way!

TIPS

T
I
P
S

- *Put technology to work for you, but don't get so carried away that you lose the personal touch. Think: 1 to 1 communication = win/win.*

- *Most unhappy customers will never complain, but over 90% of them will never buy from you again. If you don't have lines of communication open with customers, you may never know why you're losing business.*

Chapter 4

Appreciating and Rewarding Customers

Why, you may ask, should I reward my loyal customers? It's very simple - they've been putting lots of money in your pocket over the years. Not to mention that you want to have lifelong relationships that keep those customers coming back, spending more money with you, and bringing you more customers. With a customer-focused marketing program, there shouldn't be any hesitation to reward loyal customers.

Frequent Buyer & Preferred Customer Programs

Are you a frequent flyer? Think about how a program like that works. A certain airline wants all your business, so they reward you with points every time you fly their airlines. After you start racking up points and see what the rewards can be (like free tickets), you find yourself using that airline whenever you travel, even if does cost just a little more, or the scheduling is not the most preferable. Maybe you'll suffer a little inconvenience on your way to free round trip tickets to Hawaii, but you also get perks and special treatment. In an effort to

More points = more sales $

help you gain even more points and capture
more of your business, the airline teams up
with car rental companies and hotels that
contribute to your airline points if you rent
a car or stay in a hotel in conjunction with
your trip on their airline. When they send
you a statement with your point accumula-
tion, it's another opportunity for them to
communicate with you - letting you know
what other ways you can spend your money
with them or their partners. When you see
how close you are to those free tickets, it
serves as incentive to take another trip on
their airline. Everybody wins!

Buy more

You may be familiar with major bookstores'
membership or preferred customer programs. One chain gives you membership
for free, then whenever you make a purchase and show your card, you get a discount. Sometimes membership entitles you
to reserve an author-signed book when you
can't make it to the book-signing session. At
another chain, you pay an annual fee for
the privilege of being a member. Whenever
you make a purchase and show your card,
you not only get a discount, but points
accumulate toward a cash back gift-certifi-
cate for you at the end of the year. At one
bookstore you can indicate your area of
interest, say mystery books, and you receive periodic newsletters specifically on
new mystery books and authors. The idea,
of course, is that they know your interest
(because you told them), and by sharing
information on what's available, you'll go to

their store and buy. You'll also be inclined to buy more since you now know what's available from the newsletter, and you want to accumulate more points (meaning you'll be less likely to buy from the competition).

How about customer appreciation programs? Saturn cars come to mind. Judging from a Saturn-owner friend's reaction, the "appreciation" really starts with the buying process, and proceeds to develop loyal customers with strong feelings about owning a Saturn. I remember reading about the giant picnic they hosted at the plant in Springfield, Tennessee, for all Saturn buyers and their families. It gave customers a chance to swap stories and share their excitement with others that felt the same way. And what do Saturn officials see in this? They see happy customers dragging friends and family to Saturn showrooms. They see future purchases from loyal customers. They see the kids that were at the picnic returning in five or ten years to become Saturn owners themselves. By operating in a customer-focused environment and genuinely demonstrating customer appreciation, they're creating loyal, lifelong customers.

Generations of customers

On a smaller scale closer to home, you may have seen sandwich shops, card shops, and various others with punch cards offering "Buy 10 and get 1 free!" Every time you make a purchase, they punch your card. After you've purchased a predetermined

number or spent a certain amount, you're
entitled to the next one free or at a sub-
stantial discount. These shops are encouraging you to spend more money, and spend
it with them when you could go to a competitor and maybe get it for less. They're
trying to keep you coming by rewarding
you for being a loyal customer. Does anyone
really object to that?

Plan before acting

Your customer reward or appreciation
program doesn't have to be big time or
expensive. Remember the photographer
that I told you about in the introduction?
Don sent a special offer to customers who
had used his services within the past
sixteen months. The 'offer' was a actually a
letter thanking them for their business in
the past, along with a coupon for $25 off
(usual sitting fee charge) their next photo
session. He also included another coupon
for them to give to a friend. This highly
successful offer wouldn't have worked if
Don had routinely given out coupons. As a
matter of fact, he had never given out
coupons. How would you feel if you had
been a customer of Don's and paid full
price, then saw a non-customer get a $25-
off coupon? You see, his customers recognized that this really was a value to them,
and was offered in appreciation for their
business.

Which reminds me to caution you here:
don't forget your existing customers when
trying to attract new business! (After all,
that's what this book is all about!) A friend

of mine saw a coupon in the phone book from her hairdresser offering a discount to new customers. She was not only hurt, but angry! She had been a loyal customer of this hairdresser for over ten years, and was never recognized or rewarded for this loyalty. Avoid hurt feelings and angry customers - plan your customer program before deciding on your campaign to attract new business.

Handling Complaints

The flip side of a customer appreciation program is failure to appreciate the opportunity presented to you when a customer complains. Did you know that 96% of unhappy customers will never complain, but of those who do, 90% will not buy from you again? Or that one happy customer will tell three to five others about a positive experience in a one month period of time, but one unhappy customer will tell five to ten others about a negative experience in one week? As you can see, or may have experienced yourself, improperly handling complaints (or not handling at all) comes out on the wrong side of the statistics and equates to missed opportunities. On the other hand, handling complaints in a proper manner can reward you with a customer for life. And now we know and recognize the value of that customer for life!

Missed opportunities

You probably all have horror stories along this line, but I hope you also have success stories. Let me tell you about one of my

experiences, and how the complaint could
have been handled properly. I was shopping
for writing pad portfolios to be used as
employee service awards for one of my
clients. I finally found the particular one I
wanted in a certain store, but all only had
one. I only needed one this year, but next
year would need five, with the number
increasing each year. I didn't want to
purchase that single one without assur-
ances that I could get the same portfolio
next year. After numerous discussions with
salespeople and phone calls to the manager,
I was assured that more were available, but
they wouldn't be ordered for two more
months. I requested that they order five
more for me and I would take them as soon
they were available. I was made to feel that
this was a real inconvenience for them. Two
months later, with no word from them, I
started my phone calls (plural - as in many)
with the manager. I was eventually advised
that he would be getting some in, but not
the same style. I reminded him of his
earlier assurance, at which point he placed
the blame on the manufacturer. I phoned
the manufacturer, armed with the style
number. I was first told that they didn't
make that style number. After much confu-
sion, they located a supply and offered to
ship them right out to the store. Then they
kindly explained that it was really the fault
of the store manager. It was still up to me
make the phone calls and track down the
portfolios after they came in. No apologies
were ever offered. No effort was made to

Be pro-
active -
make the
first move

keep me as a customer. My potential,
lifetime business offered a lot more than
six portfolios. But they lost.

Now, how could things have been different?
The entire unpleasant situation could have
been avoided if the store employees had
been trained and entrusted in a customer-
focused environment (more on that in the
next chapter). It would have been nice had
the sales clerk been more than an order
taker, and offered to find the portfolios for
me. The manager (had he recognized my
lifetime value as a customer and known the
statistics about unhappy customers) could
have come up with a solution. And he
should have gone the extra mile to make
sure I was satisfied, like giving me a discount, or handling the engraving that I
wanted instead of making me go to yet
another store. At the very least, he could
have given me a sincere apology. But I
really don't think he even cared. He seemed
to be too busy trying to run a business, and
didn't recognize the fact that customers
ARE his business. Will I go back to that
store? What do you think?

Exceed the customer's expectations

Go the extra mile to satisfy unhappy
customers. If a partial refund is in order,
surprise them with a full refund. Like at
the grocery - if an item scans the wrong
price (and you catch it), you get the item
free. Turn a complaint into an opportunity
to win a customer for life. Go above and
beyond what's expected to rectify the
situation, and they'll even brag about it to

their friends. Instead of broadcasting to ten other people that no one should ever do business with your company because of their experience, a more-than-happy customer advertises their experience positively.

TIPS

- *Your customer reward or appreciation program doesn't have to be elaborate or expensive — just make sure it's meaningful to the customer.*

- *Sincerely thank your customers. What seems to be a lost art — a brief, hand-written thank-you note — can really work wonders.*

- *Plan your approach to handle customer complaints — and be prepared to go the extra mile to win back customer loyalty. Better yet, work on preventing complaints by taking care of known problem areas. Listen to what your customers are telling you. "Make it right, make it better than right, and learn from it."*

Chapter 5

Involving and Entrusting Employees

I think we've all had that one experience (at least) which stands out in our mind, and determined that we would never do business with that company again. You read about one of mine in the last chapter. It may have been the way the receptionist handled your phone call, or the way billing personnel responded (or didn't respond) to your inquiry. Maybe it was just the indifference of the sales person, who really didn't seem to care about what you wanted. Some businesses blame things on bureaucracy, or "that's the way it's always been done." But if you plan to operate in a customer-focused environment, employees must be trained and involved in the system, and must be entrusted to take action.

Everyone in a business ultimately serves each & every customer

Not sure what "entrusting" employees is all about? Maybe you're more comfortable with the trendy word "empower" instead. In my mind - and in Webster's Dictionary - the meanings are the same: "to give power or authority to; to assign the care of; enable; permit."

When a friend contacted an auto dealership

Give employees responsibility AND authority

to request that his deceased father's name be removed from their mailing list, the response of the first person was "I don't think we can do that." That was the same response he received from the second person, and the third person (working his way up the chain of management). After frustrating and seemingly fruitless "conversations" with these people, do you think my friend will return to purchase a car, or even have one serviced? No way!

The key element to the success of any business is: people. Customers and employees. Everyone in a business is either helping to get an order, serving the customer directly, or helping support that order. And everyone must understand that the customer is providing their paycheck. All employees are salespeople and can help make or break a sale. Their actions can determine whether you keep the customer for life, or lose the customer after the first transaction. Employees are also PR for your company, and we all want great public relations. In order to retain good customers, you must retain good employees. "Don't forget your customers" also means "don't forget your employees."

Here are a few pointers to help you develop a customer-focused culture by involving and entrusting employees:

Attitude

• The process really starts with attitudes and example setting from the top. Not only is it "Do as I say," it's also "Do as I do." If you don't show enthusiasm and genuine concern about customers, why should your employees?

- Have a written customer-focused marketing strategy and plan, and share it with your employees. Better yet, explain your strategy and goals, and get employees input on ways to meet those goals. Make employees a part of the process. Include the plan as part of the initial training that all new employees receive.

  Include

- Make sure all employees are knowledgeable to some degree of all phases of your business. Have an open-door and open-book policy. Help them understand the importance of their role in the success of the business. They also need to understand how the roles of other employees fit into the overall picture of customer service.

  Educate

- Encourage creativity and utilize employees to solve problems. Having problems servicing a customer, or a process that's not working? Form teams. Generally a group of individuals working together can solve problems they couldn't solve on their own.

  Encourage

- Invest in your employees. Provide them with training and plenty of opportunities to learn. Give them the tools they need to do their job effectively and efficiently, for instance: laptop computers, smart terminals, communication skills training, or computer training.

  Train

Reward

- Recognize and reward employees.
  They're part of the company team; make
  them feel that way. Programs can range
  from individual to team awards, from
  simple to complex, from inexpensive to
  expensive. You might be surprised how
  much it means to an employee to receive
  an award certificate at a special meeting,
  or a sweatshirt with the company logo. A
  simple "Thank you" or "Nice job" doesn't
  take much to deliver, but is worth a lot to
  the receiver.

Surprise!

At a manufacturers' rep firm for industrial
products, one owner I knew really had ways
of letting all twenty-nine employees know
they were appreciated. One one occasion,
teams formed to meet sales goals consisted
of individuals from each department. The
winning team was treated to their choice of
a movie on Friday afternoon during work
hours, courtesy of the boss. On various
other occasions, the owner would treat
employees to surprises. Like the beautiful
spring day at 2:00 in the afternoon when he
announced that "It's too nice outside to be
in here working; let's take the afternoon
off!" Or the time that, with winter ap-
proaching, he loaded everyone into the
company motor home and took them shopping for sweaters and gloves. The owner's
philosophy was that everyone in the company was a part of sales. He offered to
reimburse all expenses for anyone in the
company who wanted to treat a customer
(buy lunch, go to the theater or ball game,

etc.) Find ways to surprise and appreciate your employees, and not only will you retain loyal employees, you'll retain customers. Remember, enthusiasm is contagious!

Internal Customers

At Office Equipment Company, Inc., (OEC) they recognize that employees (referred to as associates) are also "internal customers" who need each other to service the paying customers. Vice President Tricia Burke shared with me their "marble system" for encouragement and recognition. At a central location in the office sits a huge fishbowl full of marbles, alongside another fishbowl that serves as a collection for 'compliment' forms. When you wish to say thanks or pay a compliment to a fellow employee, you complete the form (a small slip of paper asking who you're complimenting and why) and deposit it in the collection fishbowl. Then you take a marble from the giant fishbowl to the person you're complimenting, and deposit it in the marble jar located in their work area (each person has a marble jar with their name on top). At the end of each month, a complete listing of all associates who received marbles during the month is printed and distributed. For example, in December, Allen received a compliment "for always being so calm and getting the job done." Monica's compliment was "for helping my customers when they came in the store." Beth's compliment was "for fixing

Say thanks

the computers so fast." The jars stay on each associates' desk all year accumulating marbles; they serve as visual reminders of appreciation. The TQM (Total Quality Management) committee keeps tally of all compliment forms, and at the end of the year, the person with the most marbles is presented the "Marbleous Award."

OEC's associate recognition program is wonderful in itself, but it's only one element of the company environment that focuses on customers and quality. Work hard (and have fun) at involving and entrusting employees. Make it part of your business culture.

TIPS

T
I
P
S

- *Give employees not only the responsibility, but also the power to solve problems and make suggestions; let them share in the associated rewards.*

- *Employees are customers also. We're all customers. Let's draw on our experience as customers to shape the way we treat our business customers.*

Chapter 6

Customer-Focused Businesses In Action

What's been presented so far are various elements that are part of a customer-focused way of doing business. Now we'll look at how some businesses use these elements. You are invited to learn from these examples. You are welcome to borrow from these examples. No two businesses are the same. Your challenge is to draw from all the elements until you find the equation that is appropriate for your business. Mix and match until you find something you and your customers are comfortable with. However, don't let these examples limit you — be creative. Give them a chance to work, but don't be afraid to change. If you're really customer-focused, you'll know what works and what doesn't — your customers will tell you. If you're just not sure if something will work, test it first. Sound it out with some customers and employees, or try it with a small number of customers. Then, pull all your ideas together in a strategy and written plan. Chapters 8 and 9 will help you in that area. Presented here are true success stories from actual small businesses using various elements of a customer-focused program.

Borrow some ideas and use them creatively

Club membership

At **Bluegrass Brewing Company** (BBC), a restaurant and brewery, The Wort Hog Club is popular. Sarah Ring, one of the owners, explained how the club works. "Initiation consists of you telling us you'd like to join, or we observe frequent customers having a good time and invite them to join. You fill out a simple application (while sipping a brew), and pay the yearly dues of $25. As a Wort Hog, you get your very own 25 ounce (4 ounces bigger than usual) Wort Hog Mug engraved with your name and member number. Whenever you come in, your mug is waiting (and you get more brew than non-members!) You also get a T-shirt, the BBC Brew News newsletter, and invitations to monthly Wort Hog meetings, special events, and other bargains. In case you're wondering, it's called 'Wort Hog' because beer is called 'wort' before it's fermented!"

Customer appreciation

❖   ❖   ❖

Computer database

Remember the photography studio success story I mentioned in the introduction? It's time for a few details. Don Morgan, owner of **Morgan's Photography**, celebrated 25 years in business last year, which is no small feat. (On a national level, only 1% of photography studios succeed that long.) Don had been successful by doing a good job and relying on word-of-mouth referrals from satisfied customers. He had also been rather innovative with Yellow Pages advertising, and done some direct mail campaigns using purchased or rented lists.

Direct mail

But times change, and for the 25 year anniversary, he wanted to do something different. For the past 2 years, Don had been building his own computer database of customers. Now he was ready for a direct mail campaign to customers that had photos done within the past 16 months. He further qualified the list by limiting it to customers that had spent over $180 on childrens' pictures. Using their company computer, Don and his staff created a letter with coupons for the mailing. Keep in mind that Don had never used coupons before. Since it was the 25th anniversary, the coupon offered the customer a $25 discount (normal price of the sitting fee). A second coupon was included for the customer to pass along to a friend. Well, the response was fantastic! This direct mailer cost less than $300 to create and mail. Yet it yielded over $25,000 in sales, and brought in 16-17 new customers. On the average, customers spent $60 more than on their previous visit. Needless to say, Don is happily planning a customer-focused strategy for the future.

Coupons

❖ ❖ ❖

Linda Bader is one of those wonderful, energetic, enthusiastic, and successful small business owners. **Bader Music Village** offers lessons on piano and other musical instruments, and sells pianos, sheet music, and lots of other neat music-related items. With Linda and a small staff teaching a high number of adult students, it's a little easier to get to know some

The personal touch

Newsletter

customers on a one-to-one basis. I don't
think Linda consciously set out to develop a
customer-focused strategy, but it's embed-
ded in the entire way she does business. It's
a combination of a lot of little things, what
I'd call a soft-touch marketing approach.
There are the sunflower seeds she gives to
students to plant, plus candy on holidays.
She arranges day trips to local places of
interest for her customers and staff. She's
always sending thank-you notes - for gifts
her students bring, for becoming a new
customer, for making a special purchase.
Her quarterly newsletter is informative
and personal, filled with teacher profiles,
what's going on in the community, recipes,
personal notes, music events, tips, and new
products or services available at Bader
Music Village. Linda also donates gift
certificates for lessons to worthy events,
one of which my husband was lucky enough
to win for me. Of course, once I started
taking lessons, I just had to purchase a
piano from Bader Music Village. And sheet
music. And some of the music tapes that
Linda created (and that kept me enter-
tained while writing this book). I've purchased lots of her tapes to give to family
and friends, to share the pleasure. Not to
mention that I brag about her teaching
skills every chance I get, and refer others
to her music village. Creating music is a
lifelong learning process, and Linda contin-
ues to create lifelong customers.

*Thank-you
notes*

The first time you visit Sally Tyler's **Encore Hair** salon, your name, address and phone number go into her computer database. After your visit, you receive a phone call asking if you were pleased with their services or have any comments. The person calling is somewhat of a customer service representative - not Sally, not your hair stylist - making it a little bit easier for you to be honest and open with your comments. If you haven't returned in three months or so, you'll receive a phone call to see if there's a problem. Once you're a customer and you refer a new customer, you receive a printed thank you card with $5 off your next visit. Sally's friendly and very capable operators are employees. And they're happy employees who are obviously focused on pleasing customers; even with the salon's policy that no gratuities are accepted. Sally's always trying to learn from her customers and improve. She conducts surveys, both phone and written. A recent card survey, which awarded gifts for completing and returning the card, came back with such glowing appraisals that Sally couldn't believe they're doing everything so perfect! When Sally related this at a business association meeting and asked for ideas on conducting surveys, Regina Heun of National City Bank came to her rescue. Regina related something that has worked for the bank: instead of a rating system or open-ended comments to find out what's wrong, ask for one or two ideas on specific ways to improve. Each entry could qualify for a drawing for a nice

Follow-up phone calls

Referral gift certificates

*Surveys &
contests*

prize. This way, Regina suggested, you stand a chance of not only picking up new ideas, but also finding out your problem areas. Not that Sally has any problem areas of concern. She's always finding ways to "wow" customers. During Valentine's week, customers were invited to draw a card from a deck of playing cards. Any "heart" card drawn made you an instant winner of a small bottle of cologne or some other neat treat. It's no wonder that customers continue to return to Encore Hair time and time again.

WRKA Radio has a little bit different situation with "customers." In radio, the paying customers are those advertising on the station. But those customers wouldn't be advertising unless the station had plenty of listeners. Listeners are the radio station - there would be no station without them. So, not only does the station have to service their customers, they have be inventive in attracting and keeping listeners, and getting listeners to support their advertisers. That's where WRKA, an oldies stations, pulls it all together with Listener Services. This service was started in order to have constant interaction with listeners, build relationships, and team with advertisers. WRKA listeners are frequently reminded to TALK TO US - phone a certain number for Listener Services. With a phone call and the touch of a button, you have a variety of menu items to choose from:

*Open lines
of
communica-
tion*

*#1 Join the Listener Advantage
     Club*

#2 Happenings around Louisville

#3 Breakfast Bunch line

#4 Fax on demand

#5 Environmental tips line

#6 Travel line

#7 Lost oldie hotline

#8 Comments and suggestions

Some of the items merit further detail.
When you punch #1 to join the Listener
Advantage Club, you are invited to answer
a short, voice recorded survey requesting
your name, address, day phone, night
phone, and birth date. Then the recording
explains that you will be receiving a membership kit in the mail. The kit contains a
credit card-like membership card entitling
you to special offers, exclusive contests, and
fun events. The card has a bar code that
can be scanned, and information can be tied
in with a database to track your usage and
preferences - allowing WRKA in the future
to customize their offerings to you. For
joining the club, you also receive a coupon
good for a free entree at a nice restaurant,
along with free admission to the Louisville
Science Center.

*Club
membership*

Program Director Fred North is also putting other new technologies to use. If you
press #4 on the menu when you call, you're

Fax-on-demand

connected with a fax-on-demand system. This system allows callers to immediately receive information from the station via fax. For example, the morning radio deejay invites you to call the fax system and receive coupons you can use for lunch today. You phone, punch in your fax machine number, hang up, and the faxed coupons come to you immediately. Not only does this benefit the listener, but advertisers benefit, and WRKA puts their logo in business offices.

Giving customers and listeners even more ways to communicate, WRKA has a voice mail system, and is preparing to put a home page on the Web. Fred North's goals for listeners are to have fun, enjoy great music, save money, and make life easier. Fred states that "Constant interaction is important for any business." He believes in the need to build loyalty, and in "being customer-focused and competition aware."

Home page on the Web

Flexible Materials, Inc. recently announced their presence to the world by putting a home page on the World Wide Web. Mike DiGiuro, Vice President of Marketing, found that the total cost for a year would be less than one-half the cost of an ad campaign in a trade publication. So the decision was made to use part of the advertising budget to try a home page (actually it's five pages) for one year as an experiment. Plus, their direct competitors are not on the Web - yet. Flexible Materials is a manufacturer of wood veneer products, with industrial accounts and wholesale distributors spread all over the country. Their home page invites you to browse through their products, with the option of "signing a guest book." Anyone who signs the guest book later receives general information about the company and its products in the mail. Visitors to the page also have the option of sending e-mail directly to Flexible Materials, asking questions or requesting specific information. After one month of operation, Mike knows that the page receives six to eight visits per day. Of course, not everyone signs the guest book, but some very specific inquiries have been received. At this point, Mike's not really sure of the impact on existing customers. He doesn't think that most customers are actively "cruising the Net." However, Flexible Materials is trying to make customers aware by placing stickers on envelopes and statements - inviting them to "Visit our Web Site" and giving the address. Orders are not currently transacted through the home page, but that is certainly one option. It serves more as an information source (as do the majority of home pages). Visitors to the page can "link" with certain equipment manufacturers and "Wood Web" (a collection of wood-related products) for other information. Mike is already planning to provide additional links, and update the guest book in order to collect more qualifying information on the

An information source

visitors. He recognizes that this experimental home page is just one marketing tool out of many; still, it will be interesting to quantify the results at the end of one year.

H&H Systems and Design Inc., a small business located in New Albany, Indiana, has a national market but not a national advertising budget. How have they managed to be successful for 25 years? This family-owned company evolved over the years as their customers' needs evolved. What started as a local electrical contracting firm is today a national design/build firm (architects, planners and builders) of healthcare facilities, specializing in hospitals' diagnostic imaging and radiation treatment facilities. The company culture is entirely people-focused: employees and customers. Example-setting comes from the top, as it should, by owners Bill and Mary Lou Heinz and two of their sons in the business, Frank and Bill Jr. Teamwork accurately describes the environment at H&H. Employees really are involved, empowered, appreciated, and focused on serving the customer. They are well trained and encouraged with opportunities for further learning. The full staff is involved every Monday morning in a one-hour briefing. Milestone years of service with the company are recognized in an annual awards celebration. Company logo items, such as lapel pins, jackets, sweatshirts, and portfolios, are distributed and worn or used with pride.

Involving & appreciating employees

Customers and vendors are treated with the respect they deserve, from the way their phone calls are answered to the manner in which invoices and payments are processed. Doing an excellent job, and listening to and learning from customers has helped them evolve and grow. In order to communicate with customers, in addition to their direct sales effort, they utilize both traditional methods and new technology. They mail a quarterly newsletter featuring 'get to know us' articles, tips that are pertinent to the readers' job, and project news. Staying up with technology is proving beneficial to customers. Moving recently from an internal e-mail system to an on-line e-mail system has given the customer one more option in the communication process. It has also proved to be a big time saver and speeds up response to customers, with the ability to quickly transmit architectural drawings, spreadsheets, and other documents with the click of a mouse. Clearly, the customer and employee-focused culture at H&H has proved pivotal to their success.

Newsletter

On-line e-mail

TIP

- *It's all the little things you do that add up to a successful customer-focused program, but organizing and planning all those "little things" are essential.*

Chapter 7

Customer-Focused Businesses That Could Be

The Cosmetics Store

Ladies, you know the stores I'm referring to - where you get a 'make-over' session, and they record every type of cleanser, moisturizer, and make-up (their brand, of course) that was used in the process. Then you buy one or two items to get you started. What happens then? Maybe you get a post card in the mail during your birthday month offering you a special discount for your birthday. What happened to all that good information they collected that's specific to your needs as a customer? You probably stuffed your copy away in a junk drawer never to be found again. But just imagine how they could use their information to keep you as a lifetime customer. With a computer database, they could store all the specifics and even calculate your lifetime value. After a couple months, they could send you a post card or phone you about the next items on your list to purchase that will help make you beautiful. Maybe even offer you an incentive or discount. When they get a new product in that's your color or

Customized information gathering

Database

just right for your skin type, you should be the first to know! I think you'd be a lot more likely to buy and try since you're already using their products. And what about the expensive ad campaigns with special offers to the whole world to "buy two items or spend $17.50 with us, and you'll receive a specially prepared make-up kit valued at $50!" You know that specially prepared kit won't have any items in your color or skin type anyway. Wouldn't it be a lot more cost effective for them to recognize and reward their existing customers, using the customized information they already have?

❖   ❖   ❖

The Plumbing Company

Remember my experience with the plumber (in the preface)? He did an excellent job, but besides leaving a refrigerator magnet and sending a thank you note, the company could have gone further to get more of my business. The plumber could have noted my comment about additional work I was considering next spring, and followed-up with a phone call. Since he installed water filters and lines for my refrigerator's ice maker, maybe a year later the company could send a post card reminder to clean the lines and connections and change the filter, and offer to provide the service for me. By jogging my memory at an appropriate time, I will be more likely to utilize their services again than shop around for the best price. They shouldn't depend on a

Timely follow-up

company magnet on my refrigerator (it never made it) or my imperfect memory to remember them for more of my business.

❖ ❖ ❖

The Accounting Firm

Just think how much your accounting firm already knows about you or your business. Are they using the information wisely to meet your needs, while they benefit from providing you more services? Traditionally, accountants have been the 'quiet people' with a non-existent marketing strategy of "open the door and they will come." These days, with increased competition and some diversification of services, they are beginning to develop an awareness of marketing. But it seems many are spending big bucks advertising while they neglect their already hard-earned customers. Did you ever get a thank you note from your accountant? Are you even aware of the other services they offer? I've encountered many current or plan-to-be small business owners looking for assistance with the financial aspects of business planning, expansion, and business evaluations. In most cases, they're not aware if the accounting firm they're already using offers these services. How about a free breakfast seminar for customers considering a start-up business? Seems to me that if the accountant had taken time to build a relationship and communicate, the lifetime values would already be in the bag.

Cross-sell

Any Business With
Sales Representatives

*Make a
customer
for life - not
just 'a sale'*

I call it the salesperson's "new account
phenomenon." It's the drive to see as many
new faces as you can and win as many new
accounts as you can - playing a numbers
game. Alas, it's part of doing business. I've
been there myself. But numerous owners
and sales managers have discussed with me
a seeming reluctance on the part of some
salespeople to devote time and energies to
their existing customers. Maybe if they
understood the benefits of focusing on
customers (Chapter 1), they would understand the real numbers game! In order to
encourage that mindset, salespeople have
to be trained on a customer-focused approach, and the company has to have a
system in place to encourage, recognize and
reward salespeople accordingly. How about
a bonus or higher commission percentage
for keeping a customer with the company
for a certain period of time? Celebrate the
anniversary date of when the customer
first started doing business with your
company! Or a special recognition or award
when the salesperson manages to sell
widget type-B to the customer who always
purchased only widget type-A. This could
be a way to encourage salespeople to understand and solve problems for their customers by taking into consideration all the
products and services that the company has
to offer or could possibly offer (or more
simply put, to cross-sell). Just a reminder

*Employee
rewards*

to you sales managers and bosses: don't depend on the salespeople alone to make a system like this work. The whole team has to be in on the process.

The Neighborhood Retail Store

You've been in business for over a year now, and know that a large percentage of your customers come from the surrounding neighborhoods. You think you've got a pretty good following of loyal customers. But what happens if a competitor opens around the corner? Will your loyal customers start shopping price? Do you have some means to keep them as loyal customers? The fact that "I was here first and already know you" probably won't do it. A preferred customer program could be the answer. If you're already scanning bar codes for inventory and management, most systems tie into databases for customer records. Get customers to join by completing a brief form (collect the basic information that you need) and answering a few questions that will help you determine which products they're more likely to buy from you, or would like to see you offer. Give them a free gift for joining, or enter them into a drawing for a really nice grand prize. Issue barcoded Preferred Customer cards. Now when they make a purchase, you're collecting important information that will help you market to that customer and know their

Preferred customer program

Bar-coding

buying preferences. Make them a special offer to try other products or new products. Have different specials each week or month that are only available to members. Have contests for members only. Print or post flyers with "preferred customers only" specials. Give them an incentive to spend more by earning points (one point per dollar spent) towards a cruise or something really special. Send them a post card periodically with their point totals. If they're half way to that cruise when the new store opens down the street, don't you think they'll want to stay with you? Spending your time and money on a program like this will go a whole lot further than a newspaper advertisement that most of your intended target audience may not even see.

❖   ❖   ❖

The Pizza Delivery Company

Frequent buyer program

Last week we ordered pizza from a company that we had ordered from sometime in the past, but frankly forgot about. This time, their coupon just happened to be on top of the stack of various coupons that come in my mailbox every week. Before taking my order, the clerk asked for my phone number, which he obviously entered into the computer since his next statement was to verify if I was still at the same address. The rest of the order taking was routine; the pizza was delivered; and the pizza was great! Why did I forget about this pizza company? Because they forget about me. Seems they're busy printing more coupons for mass distribution. Just think of all the things they could have done to keep me as a loyal customer buying only their pizza, buying more of their pizza, trying their bread sticks and salads, and not coupon shopping! With my phone number and address in their computer, they could easily add my name. The next time I called, I could be greeted with "Mrs. Lenz, since this is your fifth order this month, you're entitled to free toppings or salad." The mass-produced generic coupon that came with the pizza could have instead been a coupon to try their bread sticks that they knew I had never tried before. I think I hear your mind clicking with ideas now.

Customized coupons

After I related this story recently, I learned about Brian Perry's experience as owner of a pizza delivery company in Florida. Brian used his point-of-sale computer information to send post cards on a systematic basis. And if a regular customer hadn't ordered for a month, they received a post card from the family-run business expressing concern - something to the effect of "Hey, where have you been? Have we done something wrong? If so, we'd like to apologize." Guess what happened? Customers actually called them and apologized for not ordering pizza! Then they probably ordered more to make up for guilty feelings.

The Plant Nursery

Aah, almost as many possibilities as there are varieties of trees. If the landscaper is invited to view your yard and make suggestions for landscaping, he or she should be

Post cards

salivating over the potential for lifetime business. Granted, their part will require listening, ideas, note taking, and a database to manage the information, but it will be well worth it. How about a post card or phone call when the perennials start

Frequent buyer club

arriving? Or a reminder that they'll be in your area delivering mulch, and don't you need some to winterize all those rose bushes in your back yard? Maintenance contracts. Personal visits for seasonal check-ups. Different frequent buyers clubs, like for annuals, perennials, water gardens, or plantings for hummingbird and butterfly

Database management

gardens. Customers get first choice of the new crop of trees, before sales are opened to the general public. Best of all, request and maintain each customers' wish list or master planting plan. (Doesn't matter if it spans over one season or 20 years, because you've got the database and inventory management system to handle it, and a customer for life!)

❖   ❖   ❖

The Tennis Shop

You broke the strings on your tennis racquet during that last match. Do you remember what tension it was strung at last time? Not to worry. The tennis shop has your complete record including when it was last strung and the type of strings you prefer. They also know the brand of tennis shoes or clothing you prefer, or the fact that you like to wear sun visors instead of headbands. How can they use that information to market to you? It doesn't have to be high-tech or expensive; as a matter of fact, post cards and phone calls will work rather well. Reminder post card that it's been six months since your racquet was last strung, and based on your frequency of play, every three months is recommended. Or that your favorite shoes have been discontinued, but they've got two pairs in your size that they'll keep in stock just for you. Notice that they just received new sun visors advertised as 'no-headache' and they know that's something you'll like. Note card offering congratulations on your tournament win, and "P.S. The spring shipment of your favorite brand of clothing is due to arrive next week."

Post cards

Phone calls

❖ ❖ ❖

The Equipment Sales and Service Contractor

Hard to stand out from the competitors? Too many "here today, gone tomorrow" contractors around? Give your customers reasons be loyal. I'll play the customer and describe what would be nice and not-so-nice. In the nice category: Receiving reminders when it's time to have my equipment serviced. Not having to answer

Whole-system approach

Employee training & involvement

endless questions when I call, because the person I'm speaking with has my complete records on the computer screen in front of them. Knowing that the technician that's coming today has the history of my equipment installation and service records. Knowing that my preferred customer status means you'll put me ahead of a first-time caller. Not having to shop around for related equipment or services, because the evaluation your company conducted for me clearly outlines how your company can meet all my needs. In the not-so-nice category: Seeing your advertisement for first-time customers offering a 15% discount, when I've been a long-term customer and never received discounts or special treatment. Receiving a call from your salesperson trying to sell me new equipment who doesn't know that your service technician was just here to service that same equipment that I purchased from your company last year. What will it take on your end to be in the nice category instead of the not-so-nice category?

Cross-sell

Strategy and a customer-focused attitude from the top. A hard look at how all the pieces should fit and work together, not just how a service contract should be worded or what one advertisement conveys. Employees understanding each other's job functions relative to serving customers - both internal and external. Modifying the computer system so that equipment sales records and service records are related to each other and each customer. Reading

Chapter 9 of this book for the checklist summary on putting together a customer-focused program!

TIPS

TIPS

• *Don't offer a "deal" to prospects that would make your existing customers feel neglected or cheated.*

• *Respect your customers' privacy. Use an ethical approach and don't go overboard.*

Chapter 8

Getting Organized: Developing a Plan of Action

If you already have a written marketing plan - one that you really do use — congratulations! Now it's just a matter of incorporating your new customer-focused strategies and methods. For those of you who have a business plan with a section devoted to marketing, chances are it needs to be dusted off and the marketing section overhauled. But if you don't have a plan, it's time to get organized and go back to the basics.

I compare the planning process to taking a trip. Where are you going? What method of travel will you use - car, plane, boat? What's the purpose of the trip? Who's going to travel with you? What are the schedules? What will you see and do? What will you pack to take with you? How much will it cost? What if the weather doesn't cooperate? You see, there's a lot of planning to be done and choices to be made - just like marketing. Proper planning can help ensure a successful trip, and a successful business.

The process itself is what's important here,

> *"Plans are nothing; planning is everything."*
>
> — **Dwight D. Eisenhower**

although you should put the plan in writing. It should not be a bound document that sits on a bookshelf and is never referred to again. It should be a working document that you actively use in your business. It's okay if it's only one page, as long as you cover all the key elements. My experience is that the actual plan - one that small business owners will really use - usually runs two to three pages.

A well thought-out market plan serves as your roadmap - how to get to where you want to go. The answers to all those pesky big and little questions should be provided early in the process so you don't get side-tracked along the way. There are plenty of other good reasons for going through this process and producing a written plan:

- It helps assure that all other owners, partners, managers, and employees are traveling the same path towards the right destination. (All employees and every new hire should be provided with a copy and be part of the plan.)

Put it in writing

- It makes you face some of the 'what if' questions.

- It makes you think about how to make better use of your company resources.

- If used properly, it will help you when evaluating results and making adjustments to the plan of action.

- It's a good reference source and can prevent you from making costly mistakes. (When presented that great deal on an advertisement for only $500, helps you decide if it really is such a "great deal.")

- It can help motivate everyone involved in the process and encourage creativity.

There are plenty of books, manuals, videos, computer programs, and consultants out there to help you through this process. Choose what works for you, but proceed with caution. A plan like this is not something that a software program or someone else can do entirely for you. They can guide you through the process and provide recommendations or help with research and ideas. But, hey, it's your business, your goals, and ultimately your decisions.

The next three sections represent my version of what should be part of every marketing planning process.

The Marketing Plan

Who/What

Who are you/what business are you in? Does your company have a niche (market served, unique product, something that sets you apart from your competition)? You should be able to tell about your business briefly in easily understood "benefits" language.

Say it in 20 words or less

Why

What are your plans for the business? Try

What's your destination?

to give measurable goals and timetables, such as the number of units sold, gross sales or percentage increase, number of customers or locations, customer retention rate, etc.

The Market

Don't neglect gatekeepers

Who needs your products/services, and why? Who or what are your primary and secondary target markets? This includes existing customers as well as prospects. Who are your customers, where do they come from, and how have they found you? What's the lifetime value of a customer? Who are your gatekeepers (people or groups that aren't necessarily your customers, but are in a position to refer customers to you or help promote your business)? What factors may affect your business (either positive or negative) i.e., technology, regulations, demographics, economy, politics, etc.? How are you prepared to adjust?

On the Inside

What will it take?

What are the strengths and weaknesses of your company? Answer from both your and your customers' perspective. How will you take advantage of those strengths or overcome weaknesses to accommodate a solid marketing program? What are your product distribution methods and sales arrangements (staff, independent contractors, etc.), and guarantees? What resources will you need to make this marketing plan

work? (Here's where your worksheet from
Chapter 3 will come in handy.)

Action!

What's your strategy for reaching and
communicating with your market(s) - both
prospects and customers? (Don't forget
about gatekeepers.) How will you gain more
share of customer? What methods and tools
will you use? How will all employees be
involved? What's your budget and schedule
for implementation? (Tools and schedule for
implementation/calendar are covered in the
next two sections.)

*Exactly
how?*

Review

How will you use this plan? Who's involved
and what are their responsibilities? How
often will you review and make adjustments to the plan? (I recommend a one-
year plan with monthly reviews and annual
adjustments, or changes whenever there's a
major change in market conditions. Employee input should be encouraged.)

Be flexible

TIPS

TIPS

- *Plan with a customer focus and marketing mindset. Put yourself in your customers' shoes and ask "What's in it for me?" Why should they buy from you instead of your competition?*

- *Recognize that successful marketing takes a realistic plan, strong commitment, consistency, and patience.*

- *Spend a lot of time planning a customer appreciation/reward/ retention program.*

- *Build relationships - with customers, gatekeepers, and vendors. Business is still done on a person-to-person basis. Consider joint promotions and teaming or partnership arrangements with other businesses or vendors.*

- *Be excited! Passion about your business is contagious; it carries over in spoken and written communication.*

The Tools

On the next few pages, you'll find a long list of various items, or tools to choose from for the "Action" part of your marketing plan.

Keep in mind that no single tool will be enough to reach and motivate your target market(s). You'll need to choose multiple tools and use them on a consistent basis. Base selections on your personality, budget, time, and type of business. Choose tools that complement each other. For instance, you might plan to have an exhibit at your big industry trade show. Combine a few other tools for success: speak at the conference or serve on a panel, use direct mail in advance of the show to invite targets (and existing customers) to visit your booth, give them a coupon to redeem at the booth or enter into a drawing, have a drawing for something that represents your products or services, follow-up with thank you notes for those who stopped by.

Steal some ideas from the companies in this book!

There's not much new here (except maybe a home page on the Web and fax-on-demand), and unfortunately there's no single sure-fire tool or strategy for success. What worked yesterday may not work today. Or maybe it will - with just a little tweaking. You've seen these tools used day after day. You've used some of them already. And you've definitely been influenced by them. They're the same tools used by the big guys. Your challenge is how to adapt them to your business. Be innovative and creative, but don't leave out common sense. Find inexpensive ways to use them. Always keep your target market in mind. Treat them the way you want to be treated. Think about what influences you to buy. If you're not sure of a particular approach, do some testing - like mailing two different offers to a small percentage of your mailing list and monitoring the results.

Check off what you think might work for your business - even if it's usually not used in your particular industry - then proceed on to the next section to organize and prioritize your choices.

❑ Networking
❑ Teaming/Partnering
❑ Referrals
❑ Volunteer
❑ Sponsorships
❑ Charitable donations
❑ Writing articles
❑ News releases
❑ Speeches
❑ Newspaper advertising
❑ Magazine advertising
❑ Radio advertising
❑ TV advertising
❑ Co-op advertising
❑ Seminars
❑ Business directories
❑ Trade publications
❑ Business name
❑ Tag line/motto
❑ Letterhead
❑ Business cards
❑ Fax cover sheets
❑ Packaging
❑ Newsletters

❑ Brochures
❑ Flyers
❑ Postcards
❑ Thank you notes
❑ Greeting cards
❑ Personal letters
❑ Customer satisfaction letters
❑ Sampling
❑ Incentives
❑ Contests
❑ Giveaways (advertising specialties)
❑ Trade shows & exhibits
❑ Demonstrations
❑ Direct mail
❑ 800 numbers
❑ 900 numbers
❑ Classified ads
❑ Yellow Pages
❑ Bulletin boards
❑ Your own radio/TV show
❑ Customer surveys/questionnaires
❑ Signs
❑ Billboards
❑ Fax on Demand
❑ Tours
❑ Open house
❑ Door hangers
❑ Online networking
❑ Card decks
❑ Audio cassette tapes
❑ Video tapes
❑ Telephone hold message
❑ Coupons
❑ Gift certificates
❑ Sales/discounts
❑ Grand opening
❑ Anniversary celebration
❑ Testimonials
❑ E-mail
❑ On-line classified listings
❑ Home Page on the World Wide Web

The "Make It Happen" Calendar

I've found that an easy way to organize and prioritize is by "seeing" all your choices laid out simply before you. Then, decisions on where to spend your time, money and resources will be easier and more apparent. That's why I suggest listing all of the tools you selected in the last section on a spreadsheet, which becomes your marketing calendar. A sample calendar spreadsheet follows. (Please note that the sample only shows six months due to space limitations. I recommend a twelve month calendar.) Columns may include "who's responsible," "frequency," "estimated budget," and "actual $." The last column can be used for recording results and comments.

> *"The time to repair the roof is when the sun is shining."*
>
> — John F. Kennedy

Once you have the tools listed and estimated budget, start figuring out your priorities. Indicate priorities and preliminary schedules on the calendar by using a legend (lines, dots, check marks, etc.) or specific dates. Some items that you choose may be ongoing, one-time, or on an as-needed basis, but don't forget to include them on your calendar. Some items may be an investment of time only, with no associated expenses, but they should still be identified on the calendar.

Keep it in your planner or on your desk where it's visible. Use it as a reminder and to stay on track. Record results where possible to measure, and do it as soon as possible. When next year rolls around, you'll have a good idea of how much was spent, what worked and what didn't. Don't forget to practice patience - give things time to work.

TIPS_____

I
P
S

• *Make time for marketing. Whatever marketing activity you need to undertake, schedule it regularly on your calendar, just as you would an important meeting with a client or accountant. After all, it is an important 'meeting' with all your clients, and it's an investment in your business!*

• *Don't stop marketing. Your competition isn't quitting, and changes in the market will occur. Plus, we humans tend to forget easily. When's the last time a customer "forgot you provided that" and bought from a competitor.*

Sample "Make It Happen" Calendar

Item	Who	Frequency	Budget $	Actual $	Jan	Feb	Mar	Apr	May	June	Comments/Results
Networking: ABC Club	JR	1/mo. lunch	240		✔	✔	●	●	●	●	
Write article	TD	2/yr.	N/C			●				●	for local newspaper
Brochure	JR	1/yr.	1800					●			
Newsletter	AM	4/yr.	2000		✔			●			
Co-op ads - newspaper	AM	6 wks.	1200							●	last yr. 3% increase
Open House	JR	1/yr.	1500						●		
Customer appreciation outing	AM	1/yr.	4000				●				
Directory listings	*JR*	on-going	N/C	→→ ongoing →→							
Trade show exhibit	AM	2/yr.	3000						20th		
Customer survey	TD	1/yr.	300			●					
Direct mail w/coupon	JR	4/yr.	1000	500	✔			●			last yr. 10% return
Thank you notes	All	on-going	50	→→ ongoing →→							

LEGEND: ✔ Completed   ● Plan to do   → Ongoing

Chapter 9

Wrap It Up!

Checklist for a Customer-Focused Program

❑ *Make a conscious decision that a customer-focused program is beneficial to your business, and commitment that you're ready to make it happen!*

❑ *Honestly evaluate the current overall health and approach of your business as it relates to customers. Identify problem areas and where there's room for improvement.*

❑ *Seek help if needed, and start planning strategy.*

❑ *Gather, maintain, and evaluate information for each customer.*

❑ *Be aware of - and seek to use efficiently - each point of contact opportunity.*

❑ *Open lines of communication with customers.*

❑ *Listen to what the customer wants and needs, and meet those needs.*

❑ *Adapt the necessary technologies to support your program.*

❑ *Design a frequent buyer or preferred customer program.*

Yes, you CAN do it!

❑ *Get employees involved on every level.*

❑ *Train employees on how to handle complaints and entrust them to do so.*

❑ *Solve the problems causing frequent complaints.*

❑ *Design an employee recognition and/or reward system.*

Enjoy the rewards!!!

❑ *Complete the marketing planning process and put it in writing.*

❑ *Have fun with the program.*

❑ *Make it happen!*

Chapter 10

If You Need Help . . .

Maybe your marketing plan is just not
working out the way you thought it would.
Or you're stumped for ideas. Or you're just
not sure how to pull it all together. By all
means, get help! After all, your customers
are your business!

There are plenty of other people, places and
things you can turn to for help, or just to
get another viewpoint. Here are a few:

- employees

- business associates

- informal board of directors or advisory
board

- a business competitor in another city

- library or business section of the bookstore

- Chamber of Commerce

- The Small Business Administration
(SBA)

- S.C.O.R.E. (Service Corps of Retired
Executives)

- trade associations

- local university

- computer software programs

*Seek
assistance*

- on-line message centers and chat groups

- research firms

- mystery shopper

- information broker

- consultants

If you need some outside expertise and advice - a fresh perspective or an objective viewpoint - consider bringing in a consultant. However, be aware that the "marketing" field is very broad. Here are a few tips to help you choose a consultant and develop a win-win relationship.

Let others help you

- First, try to clearly define the problem or situation, and your expectations. This will help you determine the type of consultant you need. What do you want the consultant to accomplish? For example: provide expertise that can be applied to your business, train you or your staff, create new programs, help you implement a program, or act as a staff assistant.

- Verify that he or she has done this type of work before. But keep in mind that your particular problem may be unique to your business, so it doesn't have to be an exact match.

- Recognize that you will most likely be paying an hourly fee for a consultant to share their time and knowledge with you. The value of a marketing consultant could be compared to the hourly rates charged by your accountant or attorney.

- Expect a written proposal from the consultant that defines the scope and shows an understanding of your problem, and how they plan to proceed to solve the problem.

- Agree on reasonable time frames and schedules, and preferred methods of communication (like phone calls, meetings, and faxes).

- Decide how to coordinate the consultant's work within the company, and who will be the consultant's primary contact.

- Communicate honestly and openly. Listen to what the consultant has to say, even if it's not what you want to hear. You are paying for their knowledge and expertise to help you.

Coming up next is a short recommended reading list. Now, no more excuses. Go forth, and ***Don't Forget Your Customers!***

Do it!

Recommended Reading List

The One To One Future: Building Relationships One Customer at a Time
Don Peppers and Martha Rogers, Ph.D.
New York: Doubleday, 1993

Customers For Life: How to Turn That One-Time Buyer into a Lifetime Customer
Carl Sewell & Paul B. Brown
New York: Pocket Books, 1990

Marketing for Keeps: Building Your Business by Retaining Your Customers
Carla B. Furlong
New York: John Wiley & Sons, Inc., 1993

The Pursuit of WOW! Every Person's Guide to Topsy-Turvy Times
Tom Peters
New York: Vintage Books, A Division of Random House, Inc., 1994

85

Acknowledgments

Thanks to my clients, friends, and small business owners for allowing me to share their stories and experiences with you:

Chip Cunningham, Simple Mister

Tricia Burke, Office Equipment Company, Inc.

Sarah Ring, Bluegrass Brewing Company

Don Morgan, Morgan's Photography

Linda Bader, Bader Music Village

Sally Tyler, Encore Hair

Fred North, WRKA Radio

Mike DiGiuro, Flexible Materials, Inc.

The Heinzes (Bill, Mary Lou, Frank, and Bill, Jr.) and the entire TEAM at H&H Systems and Design, Inc.

Regina Heun, National City Bank

Bernie and Brian Perry

My thanks to those unnamed individuals and businesses that inspired my customer-focused thought process, through both pleasant and unpleasant experiences.

Also, thanks to Patti Parsons, DataComp, for editing, and Sue Dawson, GetSet, for cover and book design and typesetting. And last, but certainly not least, thanks to my husband, Steve Lenz, for not only tolerating me through this process, but for encouraging me every step of the way.

Talk To Me!

I'm really interested in communicating one-
to-one with readers of this book — my
customers! Have a "customer experience"
that you'd like to share? A method of
marketing to your customers that's
produced results? Comments on this book,
or ideas for future editions? Write, phone,
fax, or e-mail me, or take a few minutes
and fill out the survey form on the next
page. Requests for information about my
consulting services, as well as availability
for seminars and training, should also be
directed to me at:

Vicki Lenz
Affordable Marketing Co.
8206 Lacevine Rd.
Louisville, KY 40220-2895
Phone: 502-495-1361
Fax: 502-495-1361
E-mail: vickilenz@aol.com

Survey

Here's your chance! Tell me what you liked or didn't like, or what you'd like to see in future editions. You could be in the next book! Thanks for your help.

How did this book help you?

_____

_____

What was your favorite section?

_____

_____

What changes should be made, and why?

_____

_____

Briefly describe any story or examples you'd like to share with me:

_____

_____

Tell me how to get in touch with you:

_____

_____

Please mail or fax this to:

> Vicki Lenz
> Affordable Marketing Co.
> 8206 Lacevine Rd.
> Louisville, KY 40220-2895
> Fax: 502-495-1361

BOOK ORDER FORM

Customer Information: Date _____

Name_____

Mailing Address   _____

_____

City/State/Zip _____

Description	Unit Price	Quantity	Price*
Don't Forget Your Customers!	$10.95	_____	_____
Tax *(Ky. residents add 6%, or $0.66/ea.)*			_____
Shipping & Handling *(per book*)*	$ 3.00		_____
		Total	_____

*Discounts are available for volume orders. Call Affordable Marketing Co. at 502-495-1361.

Please send check or money order (U.S. dollars only) with this form to:

Affordable Marketing Co.
8206 Lacevine Rd.
Louisville, KY 40220-2895